Maui and the Fishhook

Retold by Gordon Coutts
Illustrated by Chris Grosz

Maui (Ma-u-ee) was born many years ago, when Earth was still very young. The god of the sea raised Maui, so he had magic powers. However, he had returned to the world of normal humans to live with his mother and his four brothers.

With his magical powers, he often tricked his four brothers. They did not like that.

One day, Maui's brothers prepared their canoe to go fishing. They joked and laughed as they prepared their canoe and nets with their hands.

Maui was very excited when he saw his brothers preparing their fishing canoe. "Can I come fishing with you?" he asked.

"No, you can't," said his brothers. "You are a trickster. Your magic always gets us into trouble."

Maui's brothers were jealous of him. He could use magic to catch a lot of fish, while they usually caught very little. However, Maui wanted to prove to his brothers that he was a good fisherman. He made a plan to go fishing with his brothers, even though they had said no.

Maui waited until the night before his brothers would leave to go fishing. That night, he crawled into their canoe. He crawled under a big net that was lying in the canoe. His brothers did not see him.

After they had paddled for a long time, and could not see the land anymore, his brothers stopped to fish. They picked up the big net with their hands. That was when they saw Maui hidden under the net.

His brothers were furious. "We will throw you over the side and feed you to the sharks!" they shouted.

“But I can show you where there are many fish,” said Maui.

“Well, you're here now,” said his brothers. “Come, show us your fish.”

Maui told them to paddle even further out into the great sea. Soon, they had paddled further away from home than ever before. His brothers were getting scared. They had never gone so far before. They feared they would get lost in the deep, wide sea.

The brothers paddled fast across the sea, deeper and deeper into the unknown. The sea was full of different kinds of fish that they had never seen before.

Finally, Maui told them to stop. "This is the place. This is where we shall catch the biggest fish in the world."

Maui's brothers stopped paddling and started to fish. They caught many fish with their nets. Soon, their canoe was full of fish.

Maui's brothers became scared that the canoe would sink under the weight of all the fish. They spoke together and agreed to go back home before the canoe sank under the waves.

"Wait," Maui said. "Let me cast my fishing line just once."

His brothers did not want him to, but Maui would not give in. He took out his magic fishhook. He had made the fishhook from his grandmother's magic jawbone.

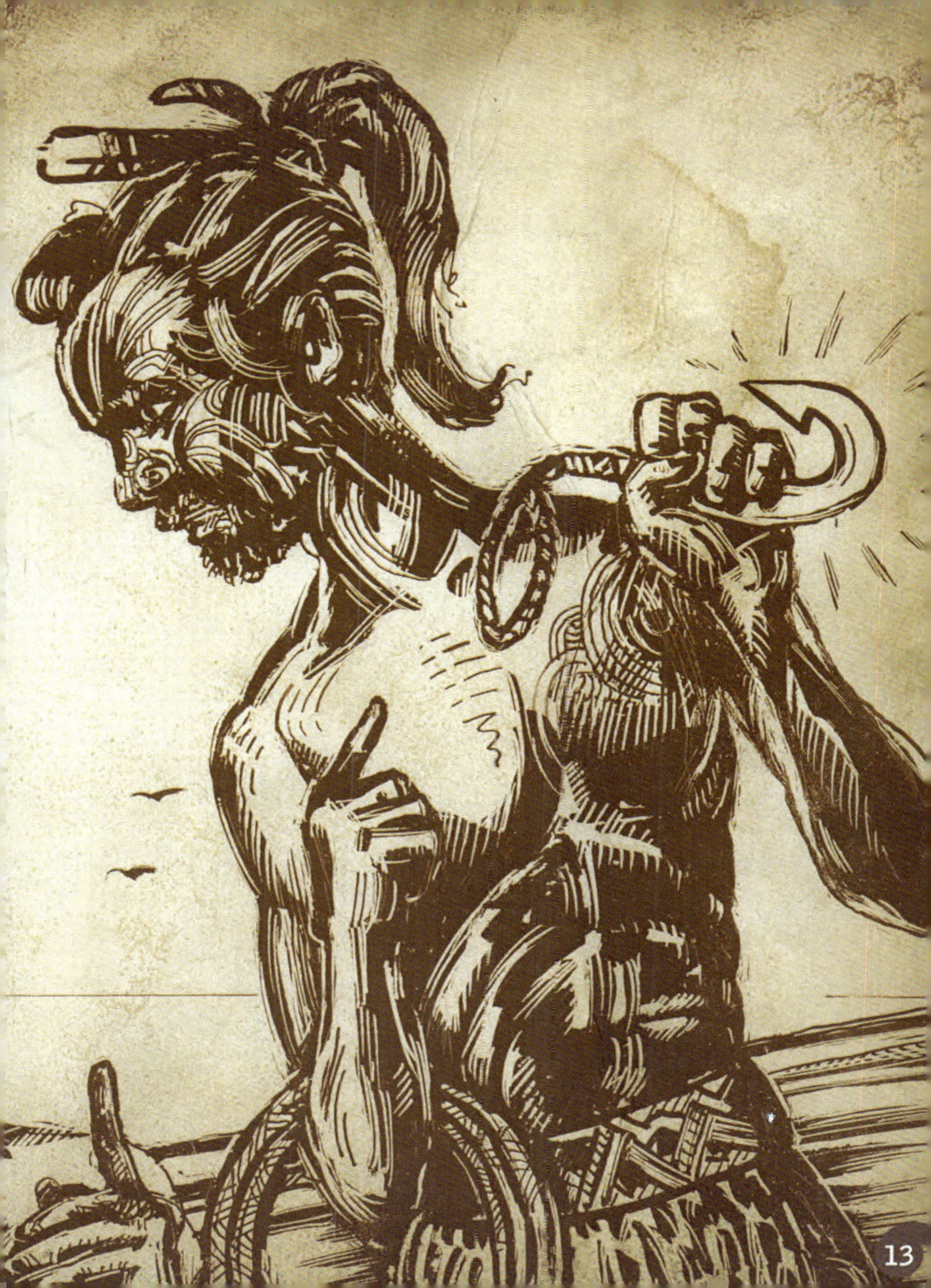

Maui's brothers were angry with him for wasting their time. They refused to give him the last of their bait.

So, Maui hit himself on the nose until it bled. He wiped his blood on the fishhook as bait. Then, he cast his line into the sea.

The fishhook sank deep, deep into the sea. While his brothers were waiting for Maui to finish, they started piling the fish they had caught in heaps in the middle of the canoe.

Maui waited a long time, sitting with the line in his hand and staring at the sea. Then, he felt a tug on the line. He could feel that it was something big.

Maui said a magic chant to give him strength and then he pulled with all his might. The water fizzed and bubbled. Yellow lightning flashed and thunder cracked. The sea started to rage and the waves became huge.

Maui's brothers were terrified. But at last, Maui pulled something strange out of the sea. It was bigger than anything they had ever seen.

It was an enormous fish. It was so big that they could not see its end. It filled the whole sea, all the way to the horizon!

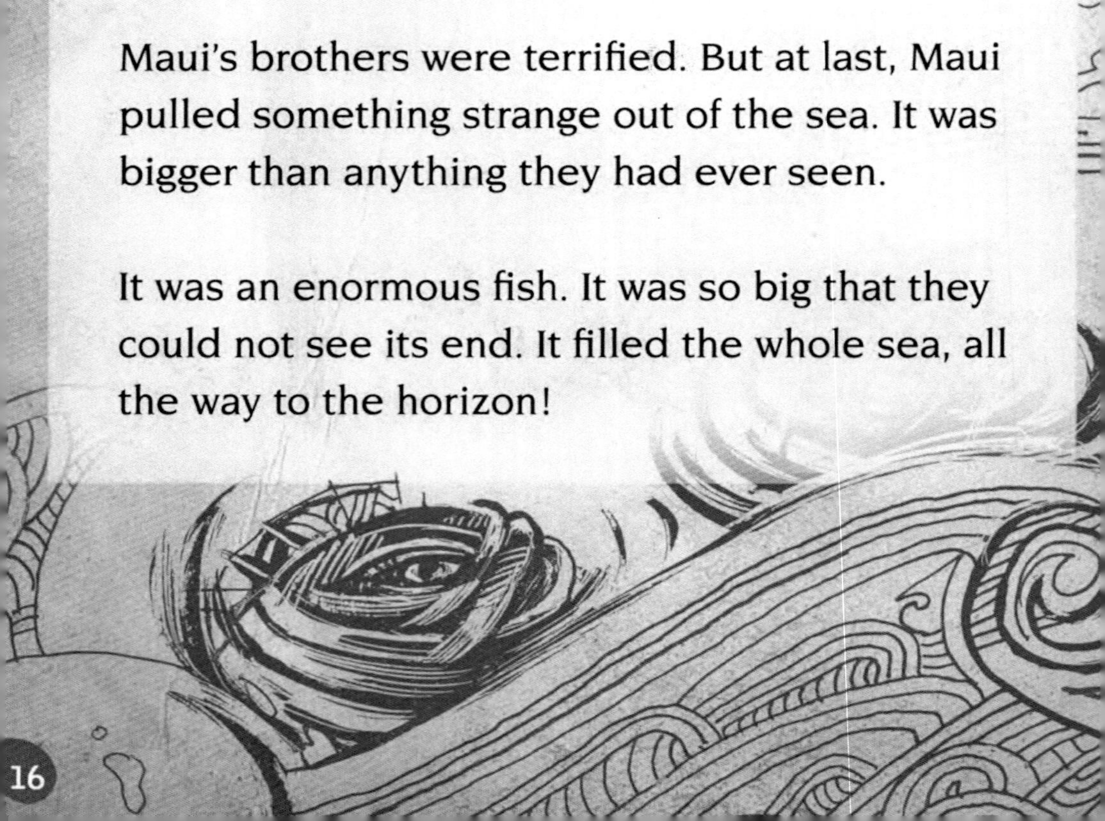

Maui and his brothers were amazed at the great size of the fish. They called it *Te Ika a Maui*, which means *The Fish of Maui*. The fish became the North Island of New Zealand.

"Brothers, this great fish is sacred," said Maui. "We must not eat it until a priest has said a prayer to the gods. Wait here with the fish while I go to ask a priest, and don't eat it."

Maui wanted his brothers to leave the fish alone. He was afraid that the gods would be angry at what he had done. He thought they would be angry that a human had pulled up a big new land out of the sea.

However, as soon as Maui left, his greedy brothers started to attack the fish. The fish raised its fins in fear. It thrashed in pain as Maui's brothers hacked at it.

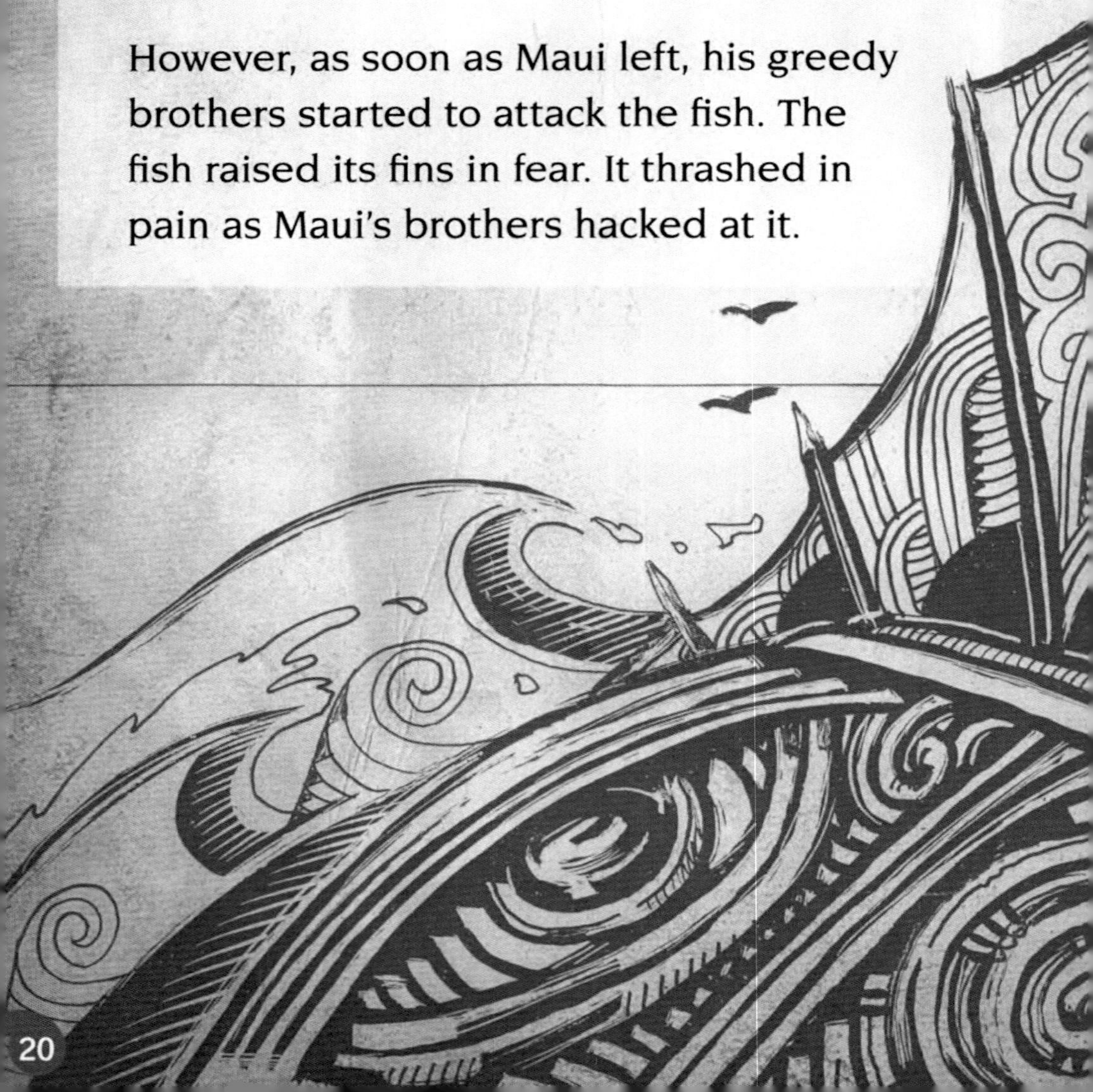

The gods were angry that Maui's brothers had tried to eat the great fish without their blessing.

The fish would have lain down flat if it had been blessed. The lush green land would have been flat and smooth. But because Maui's brothers hacked at the struggling fish, the North Island became rough and mountainous.

Once Maui had raised the North Island of New Zealand with his bare hands, his great canoe became the South Island. That is why the South Island is called *Te Waka a Maui*. This means *The Canoe of Maui*. The canoe's anchor became Stewart Island. That is why Stewart Island is called *Te Punga a Maui*. This means *The Anchor of Maui*.

That was how Maui fished New Zealand out of the sea.